Introduction

Interfaith RE is about more than just focusing on matters of content to do with individuals, organisations or projects that happen to be involved in what is loosely termed 'interfaith work', important though that be. There is far less material available than there ought to be that provides such positive role-modelling for pupils in a world where the predominant theme seems to be to emphasise religions' role in conflict – past, present and probably future – than religions' role in harmony and peace-making, for example. This resource aims to make a contribution to redressing that imbalance a little, through some of the content we have chosen to focus on.

Interfaith RE is importantly about developing skills and attitudes, through the experiences and opportunities pupils have in the curriculum area, which allow them to enter dialogue with the deeply held beliefs and values of others, in order to consider their own responses to questions of meaning, purpose and identity. This process is at the heart of quality religious education. This resource aims to make a contribution to that process through the activities and ideas outlined which provide avenues through which such things as active listening, empathy, analysis, examining bias and synthesis can be developed.

At the heart of 'interfaith RE' is the issue of truth claims, and so we focus on 'How do we know what is true?' as a basis for dialogue. This resource exemplifies different ideas and approaches, which are adaptable across ability and age groups, to develop such understanding further.

Pamela Draycott
Series Editor

Contents

Page	Title
2	RE and interfaith dialogue – frequently asked questions (FAQs)
4	Considering truth claims
9	Thinking and working together: 'interfaith is important to me because ...'
14	Christian attitudes towards other faiths
20	The same and different: respect for all
24	Islamaphobia: a case of religious prejudice?
28	Belief about God – controversy and difference: some simple ways forward

The Inter Faith Network for the UK works to build good relations between different religious communities at both national and local level, seeking to bring about mutual understanding and respect between religions where all can practise their faith with integrity. On its website (www.interfaith.org.uk/) you will find more information plus some publications to either purchase or download, including some dialogue guidelines for 'Building Good Relations with People of Different Faiths and Beliefs'. There is also a section of the website that encourages young people to get involved in interfaith dialogue – 'Connect: different faiths shared values' (www.interfaith.org.uk/connect/).

RE and interfaith dialogue - FAQ

1. What is 'interfaith dialogue' and how does it relate to and with RE?

The word '**interfaith**' operates at different levels for different people. In parlance outside of school it usually assumes people coming together who are **committed to their respective religions**, to aid understanding and develop appreciation (of their own and other's faiths). Often there is an element of working together for the good of the community (local, national, international) or around a particular ethical or moral issue (in this way it carries social and political connotations). The word '**dialogue**' brings to mind something that is positive and interactive and that develops open-ness and **respect for all**.

Religious education provides many opportunities to address **similarities** and **differences** with regard to beliefs and practices, symbols and concepts, and responses to social, moral and ethical issues. Pupils are encouraged to '**learn about**' and '**learn from**' such exploration by comparing and contrasting, analysing and synthesising, presenting their own responses and ideas coherently and listening respectfully to those of others. **Developing respect for all**, for self, others and God (however, defined or understood) and **celebrating diversity** is crucial for quality RE. In this sense developing interfaith dialogue is what RE is about, since it is never only about developing **knowledge** and **understanding** (AT1) but should always include elements of **application** and **engagement** with the religious material (AT2), irrespective of the faith tradition being studied or of the pupil.

In an interfaith group the issue of **commitment** (to their own religious/spiritual path) can be 'taken as read'; within the school context it cannot. Some come from a committed faith stance, others do not. RE aims to allow pupils to enter **dialogue** together, and with the great religious traditions (and secular worldviews, as appropriate), in order to learn about others' and consider their own **spiritual and/or religious response**.

2. Does valuing diversity mean not dealing with differences?

No – quite the opposite. **Valuing diversity** and **anti-racism** should be a part of every school's approach to its work and ethos. Quality RE plays a significant role in this but without 'reducing everything to its lowest common denominator'. Every religion contains **diverse traditions** of belief, practice and emphasis and each is **multicultural** in that followers (and forms of expression) vary in ethnicity, language and customs. Valuing diversity is not the same as pretending that real differences do not exist within and between religions. **Accepting** and **celebrating difference** is a key part of valuing diversity. Dealing with the things that 'religious people' **disagree about** as well as what they **agree on** is a key aspect of providing for interfaith dialogue and understanding in the classroom, as it is within an interfaith group. RE should take these issues into consideration as part of the way in which it seeks to break down **religious stereotypes** and **barriers**.

3. Why is interfaith dialogue so important?

In a religiously and culturally diverse world an awareness of the beliefs and practices of those with whom we come into contact (either personally or through our televisions or news pages) is important in fostering understanding and a **commitment to shared values by which to live**. While understanding and acceptance of others from different religious, cultural and ethnic groupings has increased, there still remains **bigotry, prejudice** and **religious misunderstanding** which RE seeks to overcome through the **content** and **approaches** pupils encounter and through the **attitudes** (such as **acceptance, tolerance, respect** and **empathy**) it seeks to foster.

Frequently asked questions (FAQs)

4. What can the department do?

Some **self-evaluation questions** to ask in relation to **interfaith understanding** (Grade 1: Outstanding; Grade 2: Good; Grade 3: Satisfactory; and Grade 4: Inadequate) and supplement each question with: How do we know and what do we need to do to target further improvement?

- How effective are we at exploring diversity within and between religions?
- How good are we at breaking down stereotypes with regard to religious belief and practice generally, but also with regard to particular religions? For example, what 'picture' do our pupils have of Christians (Buddhists, Muslims, etc) based on the resources that we use, the content we cover and the activities that we engage in?
- How well do we provide experiences and opportunities for pupils – to engage them in mutual understanding, in developing respectful relationships, and applying their knowledge and understanding of religious traditions to personal and community relationships?
- How effectively do we foster understanding and respect by providing opportunities for pupils to listen to and learn from those who come from the same and from different religious and cultural backgrounds to themselves?

5. Where can I find out more?

A first and crucial reference point for RE is the statutory locally agreed syllabus, faith community guidelines, or equivalent (e.g. Religious and Moral Education Guidelines, Scotland –www.ltscotland.org.uk/5to14); also, any non-statutory guidelines published by local SACREs and/or faith community bodies. The information provided here draws significantly from the following:

- **The Inter-Faith Network for the UK** – www.interfaith.org.uk
- *Faith, Identity and Belonging: Educating for Shared Citizenship* – £4.50 or free download at www.interfaith.org.uk/publications/sharedcitizenship.pdf
- **International Interfaith Centre** – www.interfaith-center.org/network.htm
- **Westminster Interfaith** – www.westminster-interfaith.org.uk
- *Respect for All: Valuing Diversity and Challenging Racism through the Curriculum* – www.qca.org.uk/301.html and www.qca.org.uk/1592.html
- *With All Due Respect: The Role of Schools in Promoting Respect and Care for Self and Others* – www.scotland.gov.uk/Publications/2002/06/14969/7862.

Christians Aware: Teachers and older students may find the following books helpful. They aim to provide resources for Christians and those who wish to learn about other faiths and meet their people. They are published by Christians Aware, 10 Springfield Road, Leicester, LE2 3BD – www.christiansaware.co.uk.

Joy Barrow (ed.) *Meeting Sikhs* (ISBN 978-1-873372-08-1)

Elizabeth Harris and Ramona Kauth (eds) *Meeting Buddhists* (ISBN 978-1-873372-23-4)

Gwyneth Little (ed.) *Meeting Hindus* (ISBN 978-1-8773372-14-2)

Elizabeth Harris (ed.) *Paths of Faith* (ISBN 978-1-873372-18-3).

The Diversity and Dialogue project website http://www.diversityanddialogue.org.uk/ provides a range of free, carefully thought-out icebreakers, energise activities and session closer strategies, together with day conference outlines to engage pupils in exploring the following topics:

1. Religion and dialogue
2. Religion and conflict
3. Religion and justice
4. Religion and charity
5. Religion and education

Considering truth claims

For the teacher

In our somewhat relativist age it is not uncommon for students to make comments to the effect that there is no such thing as 'truth', that it all comes down to opinion and that one person's opinion is as good as another. And yet these same students are likely to hold passionate convictions on a range of issues: testing on animals, abortion, war in Iraq and belief in God.

Truth claims *are* important and relevant to young people, and RE provides opportunities in which their own truth claims, and those of others, can be explored. RE also provides an environment in which listening and dialogue are integral. This opens the door to the development of mutual respect, an acceptance of the commonalities and differences that are bound to become apparent, and a valuing of these things for the good of all in a plural society.

Outlined are four activities as useful 'ways in' to considering some of the issues surrounding truth claims, opening dialogue and encouraging collaborative and reflective work.

The activities draw on recommendations in the QCA's **non-statutory National Framework for RE** and can contribute to work on the following themes:

- 3e beliefs and concepts
- 3g religion and science: issues of truth
- 3i interfaith dialogue.

They provide opportunities for discussing, questioning and evaluating important issues in religion and philosophy, including ultimate questions and ethical issues (**3o**).

GCSE and Standard Grade specifications that study philosophical and ethical issues in the context of religion are also supported by these activities, e.g.

- the nature of belief
- the nature and existence of God
- issues in science and religion
- truth and spirituality
- key beliefs and ultimate questions.

I can ...

Level 4
- suggest answers to some questions about truth and certainty from my own experience
- give my view on some puzzling questions about truth claims.

Level 5
- respond thoughtfully to ideas about truth and certainty for myself
- relate my own view of a question to what some Christians (or Muslims or Sikhs) think and believe.

Level 6
- evaluate a Christian (or Muslim or Sikh) perspective on questions of truth and certainty
- express an insight into the significance of truth claims, and express my insights into their value and importance in society.

See also

- **YBGud: www.ybgud.net**

  YBGud provides a variety of stimuli on many areas and aspects of contemporary moral debate. Why not start with the interactive quiz, 'Check your mode of moral thinking'? You are invited to say 'Yes' or 'No' to 24 sentences – and an evaluation of your responses appears on screen! **Food for thought for all!**

- **TPM Online: www.philosophersnet.com**

  The 'Games and activities' section of TPM Online provides a variety of interactive activities guaranteed to amuse, challenge and frustrate! Try 'Philosophical Health Check' and 'Do-It-Yourself Deity' for starters. Some activities could be done as a class activity, but most are best done individually, with feedback to the class. **Particularly suitable for more able and/or older students.**

Truth and certainty

Activity 1 Truth and certainty – what's the difference?

Work with a partner to analyse the parable printed below – what does it have to say about 'truth' and 'certainty'?

1. **Underline or highlight words/phrases which:**

- show what the resistance fighter **knew for certain** about the stranger
- show what the resistance fighter **believed to be true** about the stranger.

2. **Talk about and feed back to the class:**

- What did you notice in your responses to question 1? How would you now define the difference between 'truth' and 'certainty'?
- What does this parable have to say about how we might respond to new ideas, beliefs and people when we meet them? What are your thoughts on this matter?

The parable of the resistance fighter and the stranger

It was war time and a small country was occupied, overrun by its neighbour's dictator and army. A resistance group tried to keep hope alive.

One night a young woman in the resistance met a stranger who impressed her deeply. They talked all night, sharing their hopes and dreams of future freedom. The stranger told her that he too was a member of the resistance, in fact he was the leader of it. He urged her to have faith in him, no matter what happened. The resistance fighter was totally convinced of the sincerity of the stranger, and promised to trust and follow him.

Although they never met again in a situation where they could have a private conversation, she often saw the stranger helping members of the resistance. She would say to her friends, 'I know him. He's a good man. He's on our side.'

But sometimes the stranger seemed to be helping the enemy. She would see him in police uniform, chatting to the dictator and even handing over patriots to the occupying army. Her friends became angry and accused the stranger of treachery. But the resistance fighter would not join in: 'He knows best,' she would say. 'He's doing all he can. Trust him.'

Sometimes she asked the stranger for help and received it. She was grateful. But at other times when she asked, there was no help, and sometimes no answer. Still she would say, 'The stranger knows best. I don't doubt him. I know him. He's on our side.'

'What will it take before you admit you are wrong about him?' her friends often asked, angrily. But she refused to answer; she would not put the stranger to the test. She trusted him. They argued, 'If that's what you mean by being on our side, the sooner your stranger goes over to the enemy the better.' But still she would not give up her trust in the stranger.

Adapted from an original idea by Basil Mitchell, 'Theology and Falsification' in Antony Flew and Alasdair MacIntyre (eds) *New Essays in Philosophical Theology*, SCM 1955.

Engaging with secondary RE: Interfaith RE

What do people say about 'truth'?

Believe those who are seeking the truth. Doubt those who find it. *Andre Gide (1869–1951)*	Realisation of Truth is higher than all else; higher still is truthful living. *Translated from the Guru Granth Sahib*	The truth is out there. *X-Files*
Truth is not absolute, it is relative. Truth in one culture may be different to truth in another. *Peter Vardy (philosopher)*	I think God is a shining star with rays of reds and yellow. *Sikh, male, aged 12*	Say not, 'I have found the truth,' but rather, 'I have found a truth.' *Kahlil Gibran (1883–1931)*
The truth is more important than the facts. *Frank Lloyd Wright (1869–1959)*	When you die, you die, nothing more, nothing less. You don't know this, or think about this, because you are dead. Your last thoughts will be your last. You won't feel good, you won't feel bad. You feel nothing because you're dead. *Male, aged 15*	It would be nice if God did exist because he brings a lot of happiness to a lot of people. *Atheist, male, aged 15*
I am sure there is a God but I think he is just a 'presence' rather than a man. I don't believe he can possibly listen to all our prayers and I think it is up to us to help ourselves and not expect him to make everything right and then blame him when it all goes wrong. *James, Christian, aged 12*	I believe there is only one God but he has many names and forms. He never had a beginning and will never have an end. He is the creator of all and everything was formed from him and at the end of this time everything will again return to him. *Hindu, female, aged 15*	I think God is omnipotent, omniscient and transcendent. In my view, this is logical as his power has to be greater than us in order for him to control and dominate the world. The reason that people have difficulty determining 'what God is like' is that these attributes transcend the realm of human understanding. *Muslim, female, aged 17*
Life is given by God and is part of God. Therefore all people contain a small part of God and so all people are of value and worth. It just depends on whether or not they use this goodness for good or evil. *Christian, female, aged 17*	I believe that God did exist and did care for everybody. But he is not supernatural and cause miracles like some religious groups believe. He lived thousands of years ago and cared for people. He has no effect on the world and people who live there now. *Atheist, female, aged 15*	I believe in life after death. Being a Muslim I strongly believe that there is a reason for our existence which is to be honest, respect others and live a life where you help the needy and share what you have got. After death God will reward me. *Muslim, male, aged 14*

Activity 2   Evaluating what others say about truth

The quotations above offer a range of perspectives on the question of 'truth'. Copied onto card and cut into individual statements (one pack per group of two or three), they provide an excellent stimulus to discussion and support the development of evaluative skills. For example, ask students to:

select statements in response to the following:
- These questions are all true for the people who said them. Which ones are also true for you, and why?
- What parts do you agree with and disagree with in the statements these people have made? Why?

talk about and feed back to the class a response to the following:
- Is it possible for a statement to be true for one person and not true for another? How?
- What does it mean when you say something is 'true'? How do you 'know' that it is 'true'?

10 questions about religion and truth

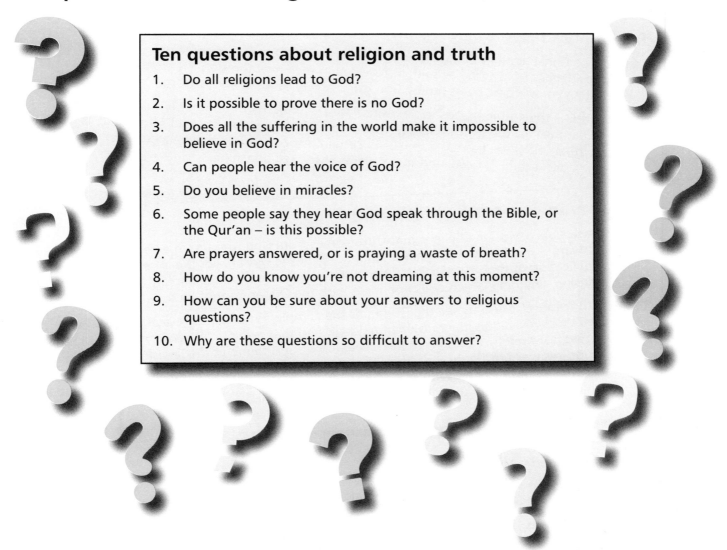

Ten questions about religion and truth

1. Do all religions lead to God?
2. Is it possible to prove there is no God?
3. Does all the suffering in the world make it impossible to believe in God?
4. Can people hear the voice of God?
5. Do you believe in miracles?
6. Some people say they hear God speak through the Bible, or the Qur'an – is this possible?
7. Are prayers answered, or is praying a waste of breath?
8. How do you know you're not dreaming at this moment?
9. How can you be sure about your answers to religious questions?
10. Why are these questions so difficult to answer?

Activity 3   Responding to questions about religion and truth

This activity provides a structure for discussion within which all students can respond individually (and anonymously) and then work collaboratively to summarise and present the outcomes.

- **Preparation.** Write up the 10 'big' questions from the box above on 10 big sheets of paper (e.g. flip-chart size). These are focused on religious-truth seeking and Christianity, but can be adapted to other faith perspectives.

- **Individual work.** Give pupils five (or more) 'Post-its'. Ask them to begin by **writing their ideas and opinions** about at least five of the questions on the notes, anonymously, and then to stick these on the top half of the big sheet of paper which relates to their question. Then allow time, maybe 10 minutes, for them to **inspect the ideas and views of others**. Ask each pupil to **graffiti at least three reactions**, further questions or comments onto the bottom half of the sheets.

- **Group work.** Give small groups (two to four) one of the 10 sheets, and ask them to **summarise** the points made, **report back** briefly to the class, and **draw any conclusions**. Provide a writing frame for each student to enable them to note down the key points raised in their group (e.g. Points for; Points against; Summary; My own thoughts).

- **Feedback.** Once each group has completed this task, each group chooses one person as an '**envoy**'. The envoy visits a new group to summarise the work of their own group and to find out what the new group had to say about their given question. The envoy then returns to the original group and reports back.

- **Reflection.** During the plenary, or for homework, students could complete the '**My own thoughts**' section of the writing frame, drawing on their notes, and their own ideas and questions.

People of faith – what do they say?

Trevor – a Christian viewpoint

Basics As a Christian, if I'm trying to work out what is true there are three ways in which I can look for evidence: what God has said, as revealed in the Bible; through the combined wisdom of the Christian community; by using my God-given ability to think and reason.

Other faiths I think there needs to be respect for the integrity of another faith, but in which each faith argues for the truth of its own position. I would want to say that Christianity is true and that other faiths are therefore untrue in certain respects, but I would expect them to say the same, and I don't think it need lead to problems in our relationship.

Imran – a Muslim viewpoint

Basics As a Muslim I believe that truth comes from God, through messengers from Adam onwards, and finally through Muhammad ﷺ in the Qur'an. For the interpretation and application of that truth in particular situations we look to the Shari'ah, Muslim law. For a Muslim, anything which does not agree with the Qur'an cannot be true.

Other faiths Muslims see the Qur'an as the completion of God's revelation. However, there was revelation before Muhammad ﷺ and that revelation was also true. A Muslim would not therefore claim that the revelation of God found in the Jewish and Christian scriptures was untrue, or even that it was only partially true. What a Muslim might question is the accuracy with which these revelations were recorded, or the interpretation which is placed upon them by those who write them down.

Virpal – a Sikh viewpoint

Basics Sikhs believe that there are three different sources of the gift of truth: God; the Guru Granth Sahib; the sadhsangat (congregation).

Other faiths Sikhs respect the identity of other religions and we never say that other religions are false. We believe in the freedom to practise any religion. People should be strong in their own faith and willing to defend it, but at the same time respect the faith of others as right for them. The Golden Temple in Amritsar has doors on all four sides to suggest that everyone is welcome. However, it is set in a pool of nectar and there is only one bridge across it because there is only one path to God, and that is the path of truth.

Activity 4   What do I say about relationships between different faiths?

In the statements above, three individuals – a Christian, a Muslim and a Sikh – offer their thoughts on the relationship between their own faith and other faiths.

- **Read** each of the statements carefully. Working with a partner, **highlight** or **underline** things that:

  (a) surprise you;   (b) you agree with;   (c) you disagree with.

- **Think and talk about**: How do these statements tie in with what you see and hear in the media? What are the reasons for any similarities and/or differences you notice?

- **Write your own statement** in 100–150 words entitled: **'What do I say?'** Follow the same structure as the statements above, i.e.

  (a) Name and perspective   (b) Basics   (c) Other faiths.

Thinking and working together: 'interfaith' is important to me because ...

For information

The **Interfaith Network of Great Britain** (see page 1 for contact details) is an umbrella organisation that many local and other national groups connect with. Some interfaith groups are quite informal and others are more structured (some with paid staff, others relying on volunteers). Regardless of size, in essence all seek to foster **inter-religious understanding** in order to **deepen the faith of those involved** and **encourage them to work together for the betterment of society**.

I can ...

Level 4
- **describe** examples of events interfaith groups hold to **show understanding** of how such gatherings help people develop insights into their own and others' beliefs and practices
- *suggest answers to questions* about why people are involved in interfaith dialogue.

Level 5
- **explain the impact** that being involved in an interfaith group might have on someone
- *express my own views* about the challenges of being involved in interfaith dialogue.

Level 6
- give an **informed account** of different reasons why people become involved in interfaith dialogue
- *express personal views* about how interfaith dialogue can make the local (national or international) community a better place
- **give reasoned examples** to **express insight** into how interfaith involvement helps in making decisions about moral or ethical issues.

Links: (non-statutory National Framework for RE) – lower secondary.

Themes: beliefs and concepts; authority; expressions of spirituality; interfaith dialogue.

Experiences and opportunities: encountering people from different religious, cultural and philosophical groups; discussing, questioning and evaluating; reflecting and evaluating.

For information

One such group is the Suffolk Inter-Faith Resource (SIFRE), a resource of people from many faiths and cultures, paid and unpaid, who visit schools and colleges, and are also working to promote understanding within the public services (health, social care, police, probation, prison, councils) and the voluntary and commercial sectors as well as providing a programme for the general public. They have produced:

Diversity: The Game of Inter-Faith & Multicultural Life, a non-competitive board game, enabling players to learn basic information about different faiths and helping them to think about the significance of personal encounters within a diverse and fragmented society. Players assume the identity of someone from a different faith and experience how that person might feel in daily dealings with others in an ill-informed world. It also provides opportunities to discuss spiritual and cultural issues and to consider ethical dilemmas. The basic game costs £30.00 plus £5.00 postage and packaging. A desirable extra is a 3 x 3 ft playing mat, also £30.00 plus £5.00 p&p. They are available from: Suffolk Inter-Faith Resource, Suffolk College, Rope Walk, Ipswich, IP4 1LT. office@sifre.org.uk 01379 678615

Engaging with secondary RE: Interfaith RE

See also

www.homeoffice.gov.uk/equality-diversity/faith-and-religion – government link (home office).

www.multifaithnet.org/ – an extensive number of interfaith websites can be accessed via this site (University of Derby).

www.interfaith-center.org – interfaith centre – they also host the World Congress of Faiths site – www.interfaith-center.org./wcf.

www.united-religions.org – united religions initiative.

www.interfaithscotland.org – Scottish interfaith council.

www.threefaithsforum.org.uk – Jewish, Christian and Muslim.

Activity 1   Interfaith events calendar

The stimulus sheet on page 11 provides an opportunity for paired, individual and small group work based around a calendar of events from an interfaith group. On completion:

- Choose some of the profiles (question 1) to read out or show – from this you should be able to draw out issues/questions around stereotyping (of the type of person who gets involved in interfaith issues).

- Share some of the youth events that pupils have devised in their small groups – looking for similarities and differences. Choose one that it would be feasible to hold in the school (such as a 'meet the faiths' session) and get some volunteer pupils to help you organise it for a lunchtime or after school or as part of a school open-day/evening.

Activity 2   Interfaith is important to me because...

Use the stimulus sheets to provide a focus for thinking/discussion about the effect of interfaith dialogue on those involved. Highlight in blue things they say that are similar (may be same meaning but different words) and in red the things that are different in their answers. Pupils respond personally to questions 1, 4 and 5 – whom are they closest to, whom do they disagree with – why?

Page 12: **Basma Elshayyal** is a teacher and Head of RE and Citizenship at Islamia Girls' High School. She is married with a young child and is involved in various ways in developing interfaith understanding both through her work and within her faith community.

Page 13: **Geoffrey Cantor** is retired but gives time to being the Jewish Faith Adviser to St John's College, York, as part of his commitment to interfaith dialogue.

Web link:

The interviews on pages 12 and 13 are available for subscribers to download from our website along with further interviews with a Sikh, a Pagan, two Baha'is and another Muslim.

Activity 3   Devising a questionnaire

An important aspect of interfaith dialogue is **sharing** what you believe and finding out what others believe. In groups of three or four, devise a **questionnaire** (no more than six questions) which would aid such sharing. This can be set around **a theme or current issue** in the news (environmental issues, abortion, euthanasia, the war in Iraq, terrorism, religion and politics, sexism, homophobia, etc.) or around a **religious practice** (e.g. prayer, symbols, sacred writing, worship). The questions need to bring out more than just what people do (practice): they need to focus on why they do them (significance – to individual and community). Each group could focus on the same theme, current issue or practice, or different groups could be given a different focus (this latter approach would work well for GCSE work on social and moral issues to provide quotes from a range of believers about different issues).

Send the questionnaire to at least three people from the different faith communities you are focusing on (your SACRE may be able to provide you with some local contacts). Analyse their responses (using appropriate software) and use as a basis for further thinking.

Inter-Faith Events – Spring/Summer 2006

Saturday seminars (Ipswich public library lecture hall)

11 a.m. 28 January — **Creation Stories and World Views**
Stories from around the world (with a display of library books suitable for children and families). This day is the start of National Story Telling Week.

11 a.m. 25 February — **Personal Relationships**
Sexual orientation, civil partnerships, marriage and family life – where do we stand? (A lot of careful planning to include a wide range of views went into this event – why do you think this is so?)

11 a.m. 25 March — **Community Relations**
Nation, neighbourhood, faith community – where do our loyalties lie?

The seminars involve listening to speakers, asking questions and short group discussions.

Events in Lowestoft

25 May — **Questions of Identity, Faith and Culture** – day conference
The conference involves a keynote speaker and workshops where people get the chance to focus on particular aspects of the topic in more detail.

Events in Bury St Edmunds

12 noon 14 January — **What is SIFRE?** Suffolk Inter-Faith Resource – *a short 'get to know us' session.*

7:30 p.m. 24 February — **Pudding and Play** – *social event – an opportunity to relax together.*

7:30 p.m. 21 July — What do the Faiths teach about Suffering? *An opportunity to think together and share ideas/experiences/beliefs, looking at similarities and differences in teaching about this important topic.*

Events in Ipswich

12 noon 5 February — **Chinese New Year** – *a chance to share in celebrations with our Chinese community.*

4 p.m. 14 March — **Festival of Festivals** – New Beginnings – *major focus on Holi – find out what happens and why.*

2:30 p.m. 9 April — **Mayor's Celebration of Community** – *civic gathering to celebrate our diverse community.*

7 p.m. 17 July — **SIFRE AGM** followed by Garden Party – *business and relaxation together.*

SIFRE at Large

7:30 p.m. 9 January and 2:30p.m. 12 January — **Celtic Mythology** (Pagan and Christian) – *meet to find out what each other believes.*

2 p.m. 5 March — **What do the Faiths teach about the Environment?** *An opportunity to think together and share ideas/experiences/beliefs, looking at similarities and differences in teaching about this important topic.*

Above is a selection from the Spring/Summer programme for one of the many interfaith groups around the UK.

1. Look carefully at the activities and imagine the people who might be interested in attending them – age, gender, ethnic origin, religion, etc. Share your thoughts with a partner before writing a profile (or drawing a sketch) of one person you think might attend any of the events saying why you think they are there (75–100 words – writing; 30–50 words – sketch and writing).

2. Imagine that you have agreed to attend one of the events. Which would it be and why would you choose it? Which one would you least like to attend and why? Share your thoughts with a partner before writing down and explaining your choices (50–75 words per choice).

3. In a group of three or four, imagine that you are part of a youth planning group for the first four months of next year's programme. You have been asked to think of four events (one per month each lasting for two hours) that will focus on interfaith issues and appeal particularly to young people aged 11 to 16. Choose the titles for your events and map out broadly what would be included in each session.

Basma: Muslim

1. Why do you think interfaith dialogue is important in Britain today?

The most obvious reason is the wonderful mix of religions and cultures that we have here. Britain is perhaps unique in this respect – especially major cities (such as London, Manchester, Birmingham). London has more than 35 per cent of its people from minority faiths – this is something to celebrate. Listening to and learning from people from different faiths is a way of doing that.

2. What is it about your faith that has encouraged you to become involved in interfaith dialogue?

For me, being a Muslim means that interfaith is not a matter of 'dialogue' – it's an implicit part of who I am. A good example would be the Qur'an and the pillars of faith. I cannot be a good Muslim without automatically respecting all Prophets from Adam (Abraham, Moses, Jesus, etc.) through to Muhammad (peace be upon them); this means I need to learn about, understand and respect other faiths; and consider myself particularly closest to both Christianity and Judaism as the two other Abrahamic religions. Imagine, every time I pick up the Qur'an, I will read stories that glorify their lives, remind me of the miracles God gave them the power to carry out and teach me about the precious messages they were sent with. How can I not then insist on learning more about everyone around me; and trying my best to create the best possible relationships?

3. What have you gained personally from your involvement with people of other faiths?

Where can I start? It's wonderfully enriching – I can't think of any other way that draws out commonalities between us and so easily builds bridges of trust between people. For me, it restores faith in the positive elements of humanity and opens doors to learning about life from other people's perspectives. It teaches humility, empathy, and is truly inspiring. Finally it encourages me to study my own faith, to look at it more deeply and constantly re-evaluate my beliefs. It's not just some vague, fluffy 'acceptance' or 'tolerance of others' and wanting to find as many similarities as possible. I think it's also really important to identify and respect differences.

4. Why do you think it is that religion can appear to be a factor in political or national conflict?

I don't think it is the cause – there is no faith that doesn't put plenty of emphasis on harmony, co-operation, righteousness, and so on. However, I think that people who are either very emotional about their faith and/or react in an overzealous way to certain world events can be a factor, as is the sensationalist nature of today's media which often give second- or third-hand bursts of opinion rather than an accurate transmission of facts about what actually happens. Another element is that religion is viewed by many as something that should be restricted to the private sphere and not take an open part in public life – some people get very worried when politics and religion appear to mix – especially in what is perceived to be an alien or unfamiliar environment.

5. What contribution can religions make to reconciliation and the resolution of conflict?

I think it's more a matter of what 'people of faith' can do – religions have always advocated peace, love and justice. Very few choose to use these valuable teachings and actually implement them in their daily lives with others, from family and neighbours through to international relationships.

Geoffrey: Jewish

1. Why do you think interfaith dialogue is important in Britain today?

As a Jew I am very aware that the present political situation is creating much anti-Semitism and the number of anti-Semitic attacks in this country has increased significantly over the past few years. Much anti-Semitism has grown from ignorance of Jews and the resurrection of age-old anti-Semitic stereotypes. The unquestioning use of such stereotypes is a major source of hatred. Interfaith dialogue challenges stereotypes about all people of faith.

Jews need to be better known and understood by the wider population; similarly many Jews are surprisingly ignorant of Christianity. By being involved in interfaith dialogue I'm trying to bring about better knowledge and understanding of my faith (and find out about other people's).

The relation between Jews and Muslims is particularly fraught owing to the current international situation. Both communities are afraid and suspicious of each other. Yet both have much in common and share much common history. Interfaith dialogue is urgently needed to break down these barriers and to enhance mutual respect.

Geoffrey (centre) with Humar Rahman (Muslim) and Cynthia Dickinson (Pagan) at York University (August 2006) for the Third Order of St Francis Chapter gathering at which 330 out of 650 present opted to focus on interfaith studies.

2. What is it about your faith that has encouraged you to become involved in interfaith dialogue?

Jews have always been the 'wanderers', not (until recently) having their own homeland. They have had to be both Jews and members of another community – the country they live in or even, in a broader sense, humanity in general. In terms of faith this means that Jews have both a firm set of beliefs and practices but also a commitment to 'heal the world'. I believe that interfaith dialogue makes a contribution to healing the world and that is one of the reasons why I am involved.

3. What have you gained personally from your involvement with people of other faiths?

Friendship and understanding – that includes self-understanding because interfaith dialogue means that you have to listen and be open to the words, beliefs and feelings of others and that affects you and makes you think deeply about your own beliefs too.

4. Why do you think it is that religion can appear to be a factor in political or national conflict?

All religions have a strong social and tribal element, which is strengthened by family ties and shared experiences. Particularly in times of danger these links become stronger and the gap between 'us' and 'them' grows. Being involved in interfaith dialogue tries to break through the gaps that it's all too easy to let develop.

5. What contribution can religions make to reconciliation and the resolution of conflict?

Religion can be a great source of personal strength which can be used both to fuel and extinguish conflict. If religion is generous and outward-looking then it will be a power for reconciliation between different peoples and faiths.

Engaging with secondary RE: Interfaith RE

Christian attitudes towards other faiths

For the teacher

The core activity is designed to ensure pupils understand three Christian approaches to other religions: **exclusivism, inclusivism** and **pluralism**. Recent research suggests that activities which involve converting text to diagram enables learners to engage with and process information more readily, and to also develop important skills in literacy such as note-taking and summarising. Oral activities which require learners to explain key ideas and concepts to their peers help reinforce and consolidate their learning, and are especially helpful for those whose preferred learning style is auditory.

This work is based on a classroom strategy explored on a Teacher's TV programme 'Christian Ethics: Attitudes to Other Faiths'

http://www.teachers.tv/subjectBlockVideo.do?transmissionBlockId=143190&zoneId=2&transmissionProgrammeId=143943.

Learning objectives

Examination specification assessment objectives (e.g. GCSE) use the following terminology which has subsequently been used in the 'I can ...' statements on this page. This is on the understanding that teachers will have explored with pupils their meaning in terms of the course.

Assessment Objective 1:

Recall, select, organise, and deploy knowledge

Assessment Objective 2:

Describe, analyse, explain the relevance and application of religion or religions

Assessment Objective 3:

Evaluate different responses to religious and moral issues.

Links

Edexel G.C.S.E (Short Course): Religion and Life, Unit A, Section A4, Social Harmony.

OCR G.C.S.E. (Short Course), Religious Studies B (Philosophy and Ethics), Topic 8, Religion and Equality.

Experiences and opportunities

The core activity acts as a stimulus for **discussing complex religious and philosophical questions**, for example about the nature of truth, God and salvation, and **to reflect on** the ways in which interfaith relations might be fostered. Engagement in such discussions implicitly requires learners to reflect on and evaluate their own beliefs and responses, using balanced and reasoned arguments.

Other links

Literacy

- Reading for meaning / note-taking techniques: converting text to diagram
- Speaking and listening: sharing findings with groups / peer-learning.

I can ...

- **describe**, by **selecting** and **organising** relevant information, the following Christian perspectives regarding attitudes to other faiths: exclusivist, inclusivist and pluralist; (AO1)

- **analyse** how ideas about the nature of truth, revelation and the interpretation of scripture might lead someone to adopt an exclusivist, inclusivist or pluralist approach; (A02)

- **explain** how these perspectives inform a believer's attitude/behaviour with respect to: evangelism, conversion, interfaith dialogue and tolerance; (A02)

- **critically evaluate** the benefits of, and challenges posed by, each perspective for Christians; (AO3)

- *in the light of this learning to* **critically evaluate** *their personal position with regard to attitudes to interfaith dialogue.*

Christian attitudes towards other faiths

For the teacher

Before the lesson ...

Have sets of the three information cards on page 17 photocopied and laminated. The activity is easier to manage if the three cards are different colours. It will also be helpful if dictionaries are available so pupils can check the meanings of words if they are unclear.

Starter

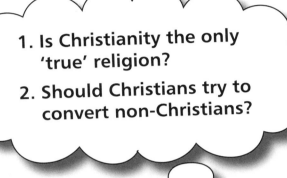

1. Is Christianity the only 'true' religion?
2. Should Christians try to convert non-Christians?

On your own: think about these two key questions for today's lesson. Write down your response to each. Try to think of at least two reasons to explain your view.

In a pair: share your ideas with a partner. How similar or different are your responses? Why do you think that is?

Core activity

Step 1

- Divide the class into groups of six.
- Each group is given ONE of the cards, which explains one of the perspectives under study.
- As a team, pupils work together to create a diagram/picture which explains the information given, using a maximum of only five words.
- Once groups have worked out their diagram, they transfer it into their exercise books, so that each member has a copy.

NB Some pupils may be over concerned about the quality of presentation. Teachers will need to emphasise that clarity is important, but at the same time you are not expecting a great piece of artwork. Making a time limit clear will help them focus on simplicity and clarity – about 15 minutes is sufficient.

Step 2

- Pupils 'jigsaw' into groups of three, so that in each new group there is one representative of each perspective (i.e. three different colours – that is why it is helpful to have the different perspectives in different colours).
- In turn, each member shares their information, explaining their diagram while their peers take notes. Pupils should be encouraged to ask their peers questions to ensure they understand the explanations being given.

Engaging with secondary RE: Interfaith RE

For the teacher

Development

- Read the 'Perspectives' on page 18. Pupils match each source on page 19 to the perspective it relates to. This works well as a homework task, as it requires pupils to apply and contextualise their learning.
- At this point, pupils should be encouraged to engage reflectively on questions which are raised by the different perspectives they have learned about. Giving time for paired and/or small group discussion will allow pupils time to explore and refine ideas, before moving on to a whole class discussion.

Plenary

- Pupils can refer back to their original ideas which they considered in the starter activity. What have they learned about the implications of the perspectives for themselves, and for interfaith relations?

Key questions for discussion

1. How does each of the perspectives above view the idea of 'Truth'?

2. How might a Christian's view of scripture (i.e. the Bible) affect their choice of stance?

3. How might each stance affect a Christian's attitude to the following:
    (a) evangelism
    (b) conversion
    (c) interfaith dialogue
    (d) tolerance

4. What do you think are the benefits/disadvantages of each perspective for (1) the Christian, (2) interfaith dialogue and (3) society in general?

Adapting this work

This work could be successfully adapted as a 'hot-seating' activity, with the positions outlined on the cards on page 17 being used as role cards.

Some pupils could work in their original trios to collaboratively prepare one of their number to be the 'expert' in the hot-seat, whilst other trios prepare some probing questions to ask of the 'expert' in order to draw out key elements of each perspectives and the implications for Christians and for interfaith relations.

Resources

Web:

www.uniwww.chick.com uniques.com/Shirts/TShirts.htm

www.sidestream.com.

Pupil books

- Victor Watton, *Religion and Life*, 4th edn, Hodder Education 2005 (ISBN 978-0-340-88885-8).
- Richard Parsons (ed.) *GCSE Religious Studies Revision Guide*, Coordination Group Publications (ISBN: 978-1-84146-190-8).

Christian approaches to other faiths – information cards

The EXCLUSIVIST view

This is the belief that Christianity is the **only true** religion, and that only Christians will gain **salvation** and go to heaven. This view tends to be held by **conservative evangelical** Christians. Such Christians feel that people should be **converted** to Christianity and so believe that **evangelism** (spreading the 'good news' of Jesus Christ) is very important. Christians who hold this perspective might become **missionaries** abroad or evangelise in their local areas, such as by preaching on the street, or knocking on doors.

The exclusivist view does not accept that other religions are in possession of the 'Truth'. A Bible passage exclusivists would give in support of this stance is in **John's Gospel, chapter 14, verse 6**, in which Jesus is quoted as saying,

'I am the WAY, the TRUTH and the LIFE. No one comes to the Father [God] except through me.'

The PLURALIST view

This is the belief that all religions are equally valid paths to God, as no single religion can ever claim absolute authority over the Truth. Many pluralists would therefore say that all religions are, in a sense, equally 'true'. This perspective tends to be held by more **liberal Protestants**. A Bible passage pluralists would give in support of this perspective is in **John's Gospel, chapter 14, verse 2**, in which Jesus us quoted as saying,

'In my Father's house there are many rooms'.

This could be interpreted to mean that there is room in heaven for all sincere, holy believers, no matter what faith they follow. Christians who hold this view do not see the need to try and **convert** others to Christianity, or to **evangelise**, as it is sincerity of faith which leads to **salvation**. Pluralists therefore think it is more important to respect other faiths and engage in meaningful **dialogue** to make Britain a more spiritual country.

The INCLUSIVIST view

This perspective holds that all religions are partially true; even so, only Christianity represents the Truth in fullness. Inclusivists would find it difficult to accept that a loving God could consign a sincere and holy non-Christian believer to **eternal damnation**. Thus, within this perspective it is possible to say that sincere believers of other faiths can gain **salvation**. **Roman Catholic** teaching states that holy believers of other religions, who are open to God's grace, may be called '**anonymous Christians**'.

However, inclusivists would still maintain that Jesus is '*the* Way, *the* Truth and *the* Life' (**John 14, verse 6**) and that Christ alone represents the full Truth. The possibility of salvation for others does not, therefore, preclude the need to **evangelise** and **convert** people of other faiths to Christianity.

Engaging with secondary RE: Interfaith RE

Copyright 2000 by Jack T. Chick. Reproduced by permission of Chick Publications. Web site: www.chick.com

Christian attitudes towards other faiths

Source A
All religions have a common of faith in a higher reality which demands brotherhood on earth...Perhaps one day names such as Christianity, Buddhism, Islam, Hinduism will no longer be used to describe men's religious experience.

John Hick

Source B
God judges all people based on their response to the Holy Spirit. In Romans chapter 2: 14-15, the Bible says that that God shows His mercy in forgiving those who have lived up to all the light they have had. Thus, it is possible for people to be saved through Christ, even if they have not been instructed by Christian missionaries.

Anglican vicar

Source C
Sincerity and truth are not identical. Sincerity is sincerity and truth is truth. Sincerity without truth is sincerely wrong. If, by accident, we board the wrong bus, will our sincerity and faith in that bus amount to anything? Will it bring us to our destination? So likewise, sincerity without truth is sincerely wrong. In life, there are numerous examples of people who were sincerely wrong: hospital patients who sincerely trusted in their physicians and died because of wrong or overdosed medication, or airplane passengers who sincerely placed their faith in the aircraft they were travelling in and never made it to their destinations due to some mishaps. There is nothing great about sincerity if it lacks the truth. What saves a soul is not sincerity alone but sincerity coupled with the truth.

Source: www.chick.com

Source D
Every prayer which is sincerely made even to a false god...is accepted by the true God.

C S Lewis

Source E
The unevangelised may be saved if they respond in faith to God based on the revelation they have.

John Sanders

Source F
We believe in the authority of reason and conscience. The ultimate arbiter in religion is not a church, or a document, or an official, but the personal choice and decision of the individual.

We believe in the never-ending search for the Truth. If the mind and heart are truly free and open, the revelations which appear to the human spirit are infinitely numerous, eternally fruitful, and wondrously exciting.

We believe in the unity of experience. There is no fundamental conflict between faith and knowledge, religion and the world, the sacred and the secular, since they all have their source in the same reality.

Statement from Universal Unitarian Church

Source G
Christianity is the one true religion only because God decided so, only because the light of Christ falls on it ...No matter how good and true it might seem, it is false, useless – because the light has not fallen on it.

Karl Barth, Evangelical Protestant

The same and different: respect for all

For information

This section is developed from work led by the Association of RE Advisers, Inspectors and Consultants (AREAIC) and the Professional Council for RE (PCfRE – now NATRE) and undertaken in Bradford, Cumbria and Leeds. Six schools participated in a project to **promote community cohesion through religious education**. Each school was paired to include pupils from varied religious and cultural backgrounds. Pupils from partner schools communicated with each other through letters, e-mails and DVDs so that they knew each other before meeting (on neutral ground). They shared:

- joint **visits** to places of worship using the *Sacred Spaces* resource (developed for the project);
- family **memories** (of how Britain has changed since parents/grandparents were young);
- a **meal** and **social event** in a restaurant.

Underpinning the project were two pairs of key concepts

- **identity(ies)** and **community(ies)**;
- **diversity** and **respect**.

Those who participated engaged in **dialogue** across a range of areas – social, theological, moral, personal, anecdotal and political – sharing **hopes** and **aspirations**, **questions** and **answers** – in order to help develop **respect for others** as well as their own **self-understanding** and **self-worth**.

For the teacher

Developing links between two schools following the model outlined in the community cohesion project is a way of encouraging meaningful dialogue with others and providing a valuable learning experience. It is possible to take on such a project along a continuum from the 'full blown' with face-to-face meetings to sending a single letter to each other. Along the way the use of technology such as e-mail, video conferencing, instant messaging, and so on, provides useful points of contact. Time and effort is needed in setting it up but the rewards in terms of your pupils' learning and personal development are great.

Links: Non-statutory National Framework for RE (QCA 2004) – lower secondary.

Themes: beliefs and concepts, authority, expressions of spirituality, interfaith dialogue

Experiences and opportunities: encountering people from different backgrounds, visiting, discussing, questioning and evaluating, reflecting on own and others' values.

Resources available from RE Today

Julia Ipgrave, *Building e-Bridges*, RE Today 2003 (ISBN 1-904024-54-8).

Result of action research project in a primary school but applicable for secondary – it sets out ways in which email links between schools can be developed to combat prejudice and promote social harmony.

Sacred Spaces four separate packages each focusing on a different place of worship (Sikh, Hindu, Muslim and Roman Catholic) – includes DVD and CD-ROM with downloadable information for teachers. Suitable for use in upper primary / lower secondary – see www.retoday.org.uk/catalogue for details.

Web resources

www.globalgateway.org.uk – register with **Global Gateway** and find teachers in other schools around the world to set up email links for pupils. (Remember to practise your school's safety policy with regard to the use of both the internet and emails.)

Christian Aid's **Global Gang** site is useful for primary and for lower secondary – there is a new facility to email children involved in some of their projects around the world – www.globalgang.org.uk.

Activity 1 Exploring attitudes to 'difference'

I can ...

Level 4

- **show understanding** of ways in which people are the same and different and **describe** what two religions say about it;
- *apply* my own ideas about how the world is better or worse because of 'difference' in religious belief and practice.

Level 5

- **explain** views from two religions about how difference should be addressed, using sacred text to support my answer;
- *ask,* and **suggest answers** *to questions, about how belonging to a religion/ denomination makes you the same and different from someone else who belongs to a different religion/denomination.*

Opening up the issues

Starter

In groups of four, pupils **identify** ways in which people are the same and different. Have two colours of paper cut into small pieces (6 x 4 cm) and give each group nine of each. On one set they write down nine ways in which people are the same and on the other nine ways in which people are different. They swap their papers with another group and use these to do a **ranking activity** in terms of most important and least important. **Feed back** to rest of class.

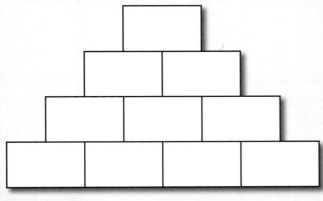

Development

Use the **stimulus sheet** on page 22 as a framework for both **individual** and **paired work/discussion** to **focus thinking** from the starter.

Plenary

On an 'exit slip' (8 x 4cm approx) **write** down one thing learned or a question raised. Hand in – these will be used to start discussion next lesson.

Activity 2 Making links and asking questions

I can ...

Level 4

- **describe** and **show understanding** of some of the practices and beliefs of people from a faith tradition/background different from mine
- *suggest why belonging to a religion gives some people (including me if applicable) a sense of identity (who they are/I am).*

Level 5

- **use religious terms** correctly to **explain** the impact of practices and beliefs of people from a faith tradition/background different to my own
- *suggest why* and *how belonging to a religion provides challenges to life today.*

Opening up the dialogue

You will need to prepare in advance to link with a partner school (preferably one from a different social/religious/ethnic mix). Decide what access to technology you will need to facilitate linking (e.g. webcam, email, video conferencing, and so on).

Pupils **prepare a personal profile** – likes/ dislikes, interests, plans for future, faith background (as applicable), what they have learned in RE, and so on. Present in an interesting and accessible way (letter, email, CV, webpage layout). Schools swap profiles and link individuals or small groups (3/4).

Read the profile(s) from the partner school to identify **similarities** and **differences** and **consider questions to ask,** particularly about any differences.

Class **analyse questions** – are they too closed, personal, general or specific? **Revise questions** in the light of discussions.

Ask partner individual/group at least two questions each and **respond** to their answers.

Individually **write** no more than 50 words saying what they have learned through the link.

Page 24 provides a **stimulus sheet** of **questions** devised through a similar link.

The same and different

Think about these things, jot down some notes and then talk with a partner about your answers	This may be a problem for the person with the difference when	This could be a problem for other people because	Meeting people with this difference is/is not a problem for me because ...	I think society needs to ...
Skin colour				
Language				
Religion				
Body shape/size				
Abilities/ disabilities				
Amount of money				
Add another difference here if you can ...				

Think about the following teachings from three different religions – what do they have in common and what do they emphasise differently?

In no more than 30 words **write** down your own thoughts about how 'difference' should be thought of in the world today.

There is neither Jew or Greek, slave or free, male or female, for you are all one in Christ Jesus.
Christianity: Galatians 3:28

I look upon all creatures equally; none are less dear to me and none more dear.
Hinduism: Bhagavad Gita 9:29

For the white to lord it over the black, the Arab over the non-Arab, the rich over the poor, the strong over the weak or men over women is out of place and wrong.
Islam: Hadith of Ibn Majah

The same and different: respect for all

"Some religions even argue among themselves – like Muslims who are terrorists and those who are not. And even in Northern Ireland you get Roman Catholic Christians and Protestant Christians hating each other. Religion seems a waste of time, why do you bother?"

"If the Buddha is not a God then why do Buddhists have so many statues of him and worship him?"

"Some religious people don't want to have interfaith relationships. They seem happy to have barriers between themselves and others. Or they seem to think they are better than other religions or people who don't believe in God. How can we respect people like that?"

- Do you think these are good questions to ask? Why? Why not?
- Choose one of these questions and decide how you would answer it – from your own point of view and from the point of view of either a Muslim, Jew, Christian or non-religious person of your own age.
- You can ask a person from another religious tradition one question about their faith – what would you ask and why?

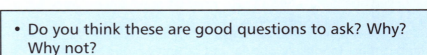

Engaging with secondary RE: Interfaith RE

Islamaphobia – an issue for RE

A checklist of good practice in representing Islam in RE

Would your school deal with Islamaphobia more successfully if these suggestions were implemented? Or are you scoring 10 out of 10 already?

1. Teach about Islam accurately and fairly. Aim for 100 per cent accuracy at all times. No lower standard is fair!

2. Use some authentic resources from inside the faith community, including artefacts, websites, books written by Muslims.

3. Reflect all the diversity of British Islam in teaching: avoid any impression that Muslims are 'all the same'.

4. Make an explicit learning focus on hostility to Islam and Islamaphobia. Consider this through pupils' own questions and in relation to racism and other forms of xenophobia. Ask: do we see Islam realistically on TV?

5. Use Islamic story, text, teaching or examples for positive 'modelling' of Islam to pupils. This can go beyond RE to include, for example, the selection of texts in literacy, examples of Islamic mathematics, aesthetics, contributions to science, and much more.

6. Use resources that enable Muslims to speak for themselves to encourage real 'learning from' the experience of the faith community.

7. In schools where there are few, or no Muslim pupils, make a special opportunity to visit a mosque, or hear from a Muslim visitor wherever possible. The DfES/QCA RE Framework encourages this.

8. Challenge the overt expression of prejudice whenever it occurs, addressing it with:

    (a) **factual information** ('Actually, Muslims are about 2.5 per cent of the UK population');

    (b) **different perspectives** ('Well, some people say that Muslims make a very positive contribution to the NHS and our health services');

    (c) **attention to the consequences of prejudiced ideas** ('So what do you think would happen if everyone behaved like this – would it make a fairer society?').

9. Use the units of the RE Syllabus and scheme of work that focus on attitudes of tolerance, sensitivity and respect to make curricular opportunities to explore prejudice and its consequences and respect and its consequences.

10. While taking account of the whole-school nature of issues around equality and inclusion, make the most of RE's special contribution in these areas. RE should be the lead subject for prejudice-reduction: is it? Do pupils know they will be challenged in RE on this?

For the teacher

Islamophobia is that set of **attitudes** and **responses** to the religion that are based on **fear**. The stimulus sheet on page 26 focuses work for pupils aged 12–14 (and allows for responses at Level 4 and above of the QCA non-statutory National Framework scale).

In 'To think about/do' number 3 you will need to give each pair a link to one international newspaper (chosen according to reading ability) (see http://www.onlinenewspapers.com//index.htm). Each pair searches their newspaper for up to 10 references to Islam and Muslims, and then within those look for words such as terrorist, extremist, fundamentalist, fanatic. They record these (copy/paste into a Word document as a record). Pairs move to fours (and possibly into eights to repeat) and then into a whole class discussion/feedback (printing each group's list of 10 would help). Then return to original pairs and answer the question: What does this tell us about how Muslims are portrayed in the media today?

See also

The **Runnymede Trust** published in 1997 a report which made it clear that in the last 20 years Islamaphobia has become more explicit, extreme and pernicious: Runnymede Trust, Suite 106, London Fruit and Wool Exchange, London E1 6EP, 020 7377 9222, info@runnymedetrust.org.

The Parekh Report: The Future of Multi-Ethnic Britain, Runnymede Trust and Profile Books 2000.

The **Commission on British Muslims and Islamophobia** carries this agenda forward. Email: cbmi@stoneashdown.org

They also have published materials.

The **Home Office** has produced two key reports: P. Weller, A. Feldman and K. Purdam, *Religious Discrimination in England and Wales*, Home Office Research Study 220 (2001), and B. Hepple and T. Choudry, *Tackling Religious Discrimination*, Home Office Research Study 221 (2001).

See also *Anti-Muslim Discrimination and Hostility in the UK,* Islamic Human Rights Commission 2000.

Some publications on Islam that schools will find helpful

Meeting the Needs of Muslim Pupils, IQRA Trust 1991 (ISBN: 978-1-85679-000-0).

Ibrahim Hewitt, *What Does Islam Say?* 4th edn, Muslim Educational Trust 1997 (978-1-907261-34-3).

Syed Ali Ashraf, *Islam: Teacher's Manual* (Westhill Project RE 5–16), Mary Glasgow Publications 1988 (ISBN: 978-1-85234-071-1).

A. Falaturi, *Muslim Thoughts for Teachers and Textbook Authors*, Islamic Scientific Academy 1990 (ISBN: 978-3-89108-006-1).

Citizenship and Muslim Perspectives: Teachers Sharing Ideas (2003). From Islamic Relief, Unit 40, Uplands Business Park, Blackhorse Lane, Walthamstow, London E17 5QJ.

Sensitivity and Awareness: A Guide to Interfaith Relations in Schools, CEM 1996 (ISBN: 978-0-85100-090-9).

Pamela Draycott, *Islam: A Pictorial Guide*, 3rd edn, RE Today 2003 (ISBN: 978-1-904024-35-1).

R. Thomson (ed.) *Religion, Ethnicity and Sex Education, Exploring the Issues*, Sex Education Forum 1993 (ISBN: 978-1-874579-17-5).

Ghulam Sarwar, *Sex Education: The Muslim Perspective*, Muslim Educational Trust, 1992, (ISBN: 978-0-907261-18-13).

Some web-based resources: starting points

- www.fairuk.org – The Forum Against Islamophobia and Racism.
- www.ihrc.org.uk – The Islamic Human Rights Foundation.
- www.muslimdirectory.co.uk – Directory of UK Muslim organisations.
- www.islamic-foundation.com – The Islamic Foundation.
- www.iqratrust.org – The IQRA Trust, a key educational charity.
- www.britkid.org – Brit Kids website for classroom learning about diversity and anti-racism.
- www.muslim-ed-trust.org.uk – The Muslim Educational Trust.

Some useful addresses:

Commission for Racial Equality 10–12 Allington Street, London SW1E 5EH.

Commission on British Muslims and Islamophobia, Stone Ashdown Trust, Floor 4, Barkat House, 116-118 Finchley Road, London NW3 5HT, 020 7472 6060.

Imams and Mosques Council, 20–22 Creffield Road, London W5 3RP.

Islamic Human Rights Commission, PO Box 598, Wembley, Middlesex HA9 7XH.

Muslim Council of Britain, PO Box 52, Wembley, Middlesex HA9 0XW.

Muslim Educational Trust, 130 Stroud Green Road, London N4 3RZ.

Islamaphobia: a case of religious prejudice?

We asked some young Muslims what they would like non-Muslim young people to know about their faith. Here are some replies.

I would like people to know:

- ...that not all Muslims are fundamentalists and keep women locked up at home.

- ...that our Prophet was a walking Qur'an, and a perfect example for all youngsters to follow.

- ...that Muslims are people who live in peace, not terrorists.

- ...that it is a religion which is clean and peaceful. If you follow the laws of Islam, there is no doubt that you will enter paradise.

- ...about our ways of living, and to compare it with their own lives.

- ...that the Prophet Muhammad was the light which led the puzzled people of the world out of darkness: he was the best of the creations of Allah.

- ...the Prophet cares for young people, so we should care for him.

- ...that contrary to some of their ideas, Islam is not an oppressive or restrictive religion. Islam does not forbid every pleasure, but only those things that appear to be pleasure but are actually harmful.

- ...that Islam is not just being beaten with sticks.

One strand running through this is that the young British Muslims feel misunderstood by the society in which they are growing up. This is not surprising. The phenomenon of Islamaphobia, **fear of Islam**, currently seems to be growing in the UK, and indeed worldwide. Some people feel threatened by Islam, and even some who are shocked by (for instance) racism say ignorant, stereotypical, prejudiced things about Muslims. This has become a big problem for some British Muslims.

'The media only highlights certain aspects of Islam. When you ask an English person what they think of Islam, they say "you oppress women, and chop off thieves' hands". What about the other side?'

To think about/do:

As a class:

1. Draw up a list of as many examples of religious prejudice as possible.

In pairs:

2. Choose at least three examples, and develop no more than two PowerPoint slides or design a flipchart page to communicate/summarise your findings to the rest of the group.

3. Your teacher will give you a link to a newspaper website – search for up to 10 references to Islam or Muslims: How many words like terrorist, extremist, fundamentalist and fanatic can you find in the same sentence? Work with another pair to share your ideas – feed back to whole class. Now in your original pairs answer this question: What does this exercise tell you about the way Muslims are portrayed in the media?

4. What is meant by the terms 'fundamentalist' and 'extremist'? Finish the sentence 'Not all Muslims are fundamentalists (or extremists), actually...'

On your own:

Write answers (or do a mind-map) to answer the following questions:

(a) What is meant by the word 'Islamaphobia'? Include at least two examples in your answer.

(b) Fear may come from misunderstanding or being threatened. What misunderstandings of Islam have you discovered? Why do some people in Britain today feel threatened by Islam?

(c) What can be done to reduce prejudice about/fear of Islam in our society? Think about what could be done, for example, by schools, the law/police, the government, Muslims, members of other faith communities, by young people like yourself?

Beliefs about God – controversy and difference

Belief about God – controversy and difference: some simple ways forward

For information

These pages provide teachers and pupils with some ways of **discussing** and **thinking** about God that are modelled on **interfaith dialogue**. These ideas don't assume that articulate Muslims, Sikhs, Humanists and Christians are available to visit every class: they are not. Still, by using some insights offered through interfaith dialogue, and some paper-based stimulus materials, the ideas are set up to enable thoughtful talking and to yield good learning. Interfaith dialogue can be bland: 'We think it's very nice that you're Jewish', 'Thank you. We think it's very nice that you're Christians' is better than anti-Semitism and bigotry, but it's fairly superficial and doesn't get to the heart of respecting and learning from each other. Where dialogue based on trust and mutuality is unafraid of real disagreement, and seeks to spark learning from the flint of controversy, then educationists should sit up and take notice.

I can ...

Level 4

- **show** that I **understand** words/ideas such as 'dialogue' 'humanism' 'tolerance' and 'inter-religious'
- *apply the idea of learning from dialogue to my own understanding of questions about God.*

Level 5

- **explain** what can be learned from different religions about questions to do with God
- **identify** and **explain** similarities and differences of belief about God
- *express my own views clearly about what religious and non-religious people believe about God.*

Level 6

- **interpret** sacred texts to **give an informed account** of similarities and differences in views about God from several religions
- *express insights of my own into the value of interfaith dialogue, especially about beliefs about God.*

For the teacher

Controversy and **difference** is evident around what different faiths (and non-religious life stances) **believe about God**. This work uses teachings and ideas about God from Muslim, Sikh, Christian and Humanist standpoints, encouraging dialogue without glossing over difference. It aims to enable learners to identify differences in belief about God.

It is designed for young people ages 13–15, but may be easily adapted to the learning needs of other age groups. The 'I can...' statements are designed to help teachers and pupils be clear about the objectives of the activity and the learning that is going on.

© 2006 RE Today Services
Permission is granted to photocopy this page for use in classroom activities in schools that have purchased this publication.

Activity 1 Thinking about learning from others

In fours, pupils begin by talking about learning from others. What have they learned through talking to or from the example of others? Who has taught them a lot? Refer them to the idea that people of different religions can learn from each other (a major aspect of 'interfaith dialogue').

Activity 2 Sorting out different views

Each group of four needs a cut up set of the cards (pp.29–30). Ask them to read two each, and try to work out which come from Sikhs, Christians, Muslims and Humanists. They need to be able to give reasons for their choices. Feed back to the whole class. This chart provides the teacher with the answers.

Page 29	
Muslim: Writings of Al Ghazali (eleventh-century CE).	**Christian:** the Apostle's Creed.
Muslim: The first Surah of the Qur'an.	**Christian:** twenty-first century CE liturgy.

Page 30	
Sikh: Guru Granth Sahib, Savayye 10.	**Humanist:** John – present day.
Sikh: The Mool Mantar.	**Humanist:** Barbara Smoker, past President of the British Humanist Association, 1998.

Activity 3 Dialogue in the group

Use the formula 'agree/disagree/don't get it/want to ask' to get each group into dialogue about the points of view they have sorted. Each person in the group must say, in turn, something they agree with from the cards, something they disagree with, something they don't get and something they would like to ask. This launches the discussion, which may be allowed to proceed in a more unstructured way in the groups, or may be helped by asking them to record and report back six points arising from their conversation. This formula recurs in Activity 4.

Activity 4 Noting similarities and differences

Each group needs a copy (possibly enlarged) of p.31. It provides a structure for developing the skill of accounting for similarities and differences within and between religions. Some are easier to address than others, and the Humanist position may be mostly identified by differences rather than similarities. Feed in some probing questions when they have mostly completed the sheet: Are the Muslims, Christians and Sikhs worshipping the same God, or three different Gods? How could you find out who is 'right' about God?

Activity 5 Learning from dialogue

Page 32 provides an extended writing frame. It could be used as an assessment task and/or a well-structured homework. Multiple-option writing frames enable pupils to follow interests and insights and provide a useful structure both to support the lower-achieving writer and challenge the gifted pupil. They should look at all the prompts and choose any six boxes from which to draw ideas.

See also…

http://www.diversityanddialogue.org.uk/. This excellent website co-ordinates information about lots of interfaith projects from around the UK.

www.pcfre.org.uk/db This database of pupils' ideas includes over 16,000 multi-faith answers to the 'God question'. Pupils can search it easily and add to it their own insights.

BBC Curriculum Bites: RE Series 2 – a very useful short programme, 'Is God real?' (dialogue about God between 4 young people) – work pack can be purchased from RE Today via www.retoday.org.uk.

From this series: *Assessed RE* (RE Today 2006) pp.20–27 for further work on the idea of God.

Beliefs about God – controversy and difference

I believe in God, the Father almighty,
Creator of heaven and earth.

I believe in Jesus Christ, his only Son, our Lord,
who was conceived by the Holy Spirit,
born of the Virgin Mary, suffered under Pontius Pilate,
was crucified, died, and was buried,
he descended to the dead.
On the third day he rose again, he ascended into heaven,
he is seated at the right hand of the Father,
and he will come to judge the living and the dead.

I believe in the Holy Spirit, the holy catholic Church,
the communion of saints, the forgiveness of sins,
the resurrection of the body, and the life everlasting.

Amen

We do not believe that life is pointless
We believe that God's gift of one life is full of meanings.
We do not believe that Jesus is dead and gone
We believe that Jesus lives in the people of God today.
We do not believe that death is the end
We believe in hope: heaven waits for us beyond the grave.
We do not believe that poverty or war are inevitable
We believe that the spirit of peace and equality will win.
We do not believe that money makes the world go round
We believe that love makes the world go round.

He in his essence is one, without any partner
Single without any similar
Eternal without any opposite
Separate without any like
He is one
Prior with nothing before him
From eternity without any beginning
Abiding in existence without any after him
To eternity without an end
Subsisting without ending
Abiding without termination
Measure does not bind him
Boundaries do not contain him.

In the name of Allah,
The Benificent,
The Merciful,
Lord of the worlds,
Ruler of the day of judgement.
You alone we worship
You alone we ask for help
Show us the straight path.

We think that 'THE GOLDEN RULE' – 'Treat other people in the way you would like to be treated yourself' – is very important. We see that Jesus taught this rule, as did Confucius and The Buddha who emphasised it 500 years before Jesus. It doesn't need God to tell us this: humanity can work out for ourselves what is good. So we don't think God is real, and we don't think we need God to help us find out what is good, either.

God, it is said, is the answer to the question 'Why does anything exist at all?' But if it is necessary to explain existence, you would still have to explain why and how God existed. So the God-idea doesn't provide a final answer, unless you then assert that God existed from all eternity, uncaused. And why should that be easier to accept than that matter/energy existed from all eternity, uncaused?

Some worship stones, some bear them on their heads
Some wear phalluses around their necks
Some claim to see the One in the south
Some bow their heads to the west
Some worship idols, some images of animals
Some run to worship the dead at their graves
The entire world is lost in false ritual
None knows the mystery of the Almighty One.

There is One Being
Truth by Name
Primal Creator
Without fear
Without enemies
Timeless in form
Unborn
Self-existent
Realised by the grace of the Guru.

Identifying similarities and differences through dialogue and listening

Beliefs about God – controversy and difference

	Sikhs and Christians	Muslims and Sikhs	Muslims and Humanists	Christians and Humanists	Sikhs and Humanists	Muslims and Christians
Similarities						
Differences						
What I think: agree / disagree / don't get it / want to ask						

Engaging with secondary RE: Interfaith RE

Writing frame: My responses to different viewpoints about God

Use the nine boxes below to select prompts. Choose at least two sentence starters from at least six of the different boxes to construct your piece of extended written work about God. Think carefully, and aim to produce a high-quality essay.

Questions and starters
- I used to think that God was...
- My own views about God don't agree with...
- Two reasons for my beliefs about God are...
- One person whose ideas have influenced me is...
- A question that puzzles me about God is...

Sikh teaching
- The Sikh scriptures teach that God is...
- Sikhs believe that God is ...
- Sikhs say God is a mystery. I think...
- If God is eternal then...
- In my opinion, the Sikh teaching about God is...
- I find it hard to understand why...

Islamic teaching
- When Muslims think about God, they...
- Muslims believe that God is...
- Muslims don't believe...
- I'd like to ask a Muslim...
- My reaction to Muslim ideas is...
- Muslim ideas are similar to those from...
- Muslim ideas are unique because...

Christian teaching
- Christians believe in God as 'trinity'. This means...
- One Christian idea I find hard to understand is...
- I agree with Christianity that...
- Christians are different from other religions because...
- Christians are similar to other faiths because...

Humanist thinking
- Humanists are people who...
- They reject all ideas of a 'great big God' because...
- Humanists argue that religion is wrong because...
- I like the Humanist ideas because...
- I'd like to ask a Humanist...

Puzzling issues
- Whenever I think about God, I always wonder...
- One difficult thing about talking about God is that...
- You can't talk clearly about God because...
- A problem for atheists is...
- A problem for those who believe in God is...

My own ideas
- My beliefs about God are...
- The reasons I believe this are...
- I have been influenced by...
- To me, questions about God are important because...
- One idea I really disagree with is...

Others in my class
- Some people in my class think...
- Others argue...
- Why do people hold such different views? I think...
- From talking with others, you can learn...
- The value of dialogue and conversation about God is...

Conclusions
- I have been changing my views about...
- I've learned from other people's beliefs that...
- If you listen to lots of different views, then...
- My conclusion from all this work is...